31 PALEO BROWN BAG LUNCHES TO GO

Easy Recipes for Working People

Mary Scott

DISCLAIMER

Table of Contents

INTRODUCTION

According to Loren Cordain, PH.D, a New York Times bestselling author, "The Paleo Diet, the world's healthiest diet -- is based upon eating wholesome, contemporary foods from the food groups that our hunter-gatherer ancestors would have thrived on during the Paleolithic era, or Stone Age." Now the talk of the town, the Paleo Diet includes meat, seafood, and an endless amount of fresh vegetables and fruit. It focuses on eliminating carbohydrates and sugar, two substances that have become so prevalent in today's world of processed foods and artificial flavoring. The Paleo Diet goes back to the basics before the Agricultural Revolution. Removing legumes, cereal grains, dairy, refined sugar, potatoes, processed foods, salt, and refined vegetable oils from one's diet is, in brief, what the Paleo Diet entails. The Paleo diet and lifestyle boasts of health benefits that include a decrease in blood sugar and insulin levels, an increased metabolic rate that promotes weight loss and weight stabilization, an improvement of most diseases involving the gastronomical tract, and an improvement of many diseases and disease symptoms including, but not limited to, osteoporosis, hypertension, asthma, and insomnia.

This book is a collaboration of 31 Paleo lunch recipes for working people. Quick, simple, and nutritious, these recipes all have a preparation time of 30 minutes or less to help you stick to your diet and nutritional goals. Each meal includes the number of servings it yields, a detailed list of ingredients, step-by-step directions, and useful nutritional information. From salads to sandwiches, this selection provides tasty options that are satisfying and portable. Get back to the way your ancestors ate. With high proteins, low carbohydrates, and healthy fats, these recipes will have you revitalized and prepared to take on your new life, Paleo-style.

PALEO LUNCH RECIPES

Lemon Salmon Salad
Makes 3 servings

Ingredients
1 lb. salmon fillet
1/2 lemon (for juice)
1 stalk of celery (chopped)
1 tsp dill (fresh, chopped)
Capful of extra virgin olive oil
Black pepper and sea salt to season to your liking

Directions
1. Preheat oven to 350F.
2. Season salmon with sea salt and black pepper and bake for 5-10 minutes. Salmon should be flaky.
3. Place cooked salmon into a mixing bowl and add the remainder of the ingredients.
4. Serve cold.

Nutritional Information
Easy to pack and store in the fridge, this salmon salad has lots of flavor, 29 grams of protein, 11 grams of fat, and under 1 gram of carbs. Try finishing off this 215-calorie-per-serving lunch with a fresh piece of fruit for something sweet.

Sweet Chicken Salad

Makes 3 servings

Ingredients
 2 chicken breasts (cooked to your liking, chopped)
 2 stalks of celery (chopped)
 1/2 cup pecans (chopped)
 1/2 cup dried cranberries
 1/3 cup lite mayo
 2 heads of lettuce (torn)
 1 Tbsp. honey
 1 tsp poppy seeds
 1 Tbsp. apple cider vinegar

Directions
1. Combine ingredients in a bowl.
2. Eat!

Nutritional Information:
Easy. Nutritious. Delicious. With under 200 calories per serving, 4 grams of protein, 14 grams of fat, and 17 grams of carbs, this recipe is fast and perfect for those always on the go. Save some for tomorrow!

Stuffed Tomatoes
Makes 3 servings

Ingredients
3 large tomatoes
6 button mushrooms (sliced)
4 cloves of garlic (minced)
6 sun-dried tomatoes (chopped)
1 tsp black pepper
1/2 tsp paprika
8 leaves of basil (torn)
1Tbsp. thyme

Directions
1. Preheat oven to 350F.
2. Scrape out tomato innards and save. Put hollowed tomatoes in a small baking dish.
3. In a mixing bowl, combine tomato innards with mushrooms, garlic, sun-dried tomatoes, black pepper, paprika, thyme, and basil.
4. Fill hollowed tomatoes with mixture and bake for 25 minutes.

Nutritional Information
With 5 grams of protein, 1 gram of fat, and 20 grams of carbs, this is a quick and easy option for vegetarians. Enjoy this juicy lunch at only 95 calories per serving.

Chicken Piccata

Makes 4 servings

Ingredients
1 cup chicken broth (no-salt-added)
4 chicken breasts (skinless, boneless)
1/2 cup lemon juice
3 Tbsp. olive oil
1 cup onion (chopped)
1 clove of garlic (minced)
2 cups artichoke hearts (chopped)
3 Tbsp. capers
1 Tbsp. black pepper

Directions
1. In a shallow dish, combine chicken broth, chicken, and lemon juice. Marinate overnight in the refrigerator.
2. In a sauté pan, heat olive oil and mix in garlic and onion, letting cook for about 2 minutes
3. Take out the chicken from the marinade, saving the marinade. Add the chicken to the sauté pan and cook each side between 5-10 minutes, or until browned.
4. Once both sides are browned, add in artichoke hearts, capers, pepper, and the saved marinade. Turn the heat down and let simmer until chicken is cooked through, or for about another 10 minutes.

Nutritional Information
Try making this lunch over the weekend, and save the chicken to pack for the week. Under 350 calories per serving, this tasty chicken bears 35 grams of protein, 20 grams of fat, and only 5 grams of carbs. Eat along

with celery sticks or carrots to get those extra veggies in.

Spicy Tuna Salad
Makes 3 servings

Ingredients
2 cans chunk light tuna (7oz cans)
20 green olives (chopped)
1/2 cup green onions (chopped)
3 Tbsp. capers
1 jalapeño pepper (chopped)
1 red bell pepper (chopped)
2 Tbsp. olive oil
2 Tbsp. red chili flakes
Lemon juice (use 3 lemons)

Directions
1. Combine all ingredients in a large bowl. Mix.
2. Serve cold -- alone or over a green salad.

Nutritional Information
Naturally low in fat, tuna makes for a great, easily packable, office lunch. Enjoy at only 100 calories, 9 grams of fat, 4 grams of carbs, and 1 gram of protein per serving. Those jalapeños will certainly keep your mouth entertained!

Tasty Chicken Wraps
Makes 8 servings

Ingredients
2 chicken breasts (Skinless, boneless. Can be poached, baked, or broiled.)
2 stalks of celery (chopped)
1/4 cup basil (chopped)
2 Tbsp. olive oil
2 Tbsp. lemon juice
1 tsp garlic (minced)
Black pepper to season to your liking
1 head of romaine or radicchio lettuce

Directions
1. Finely chop or shred chicken breasts and put in a medium-sized bowl.
2. Mix the chicken with basil, celery, olive oil, lemon juice, garlic, and black pepper.
3. On lettuce leaves, spoon chicken and roll up.

This recipe is great because it allows you to make a bunch of wraps to save for a busy week.

Nutritional Information:
At 115 calories, 12 grams of protein, 7 grams of fat, and less than one gram of carbs per serving, these wraps are light but surely tasty. Feel free to substitute your favorite meat for the chicken to mix things up.

Chicken Enchiladas
Makes 8 servings

Ingredients
2 lb. s chicken breast (boneless, skinless) cut into 1"
cubes
2 Tbsp. olive oil
4 garlic cloves (minced)
1/2 cup onion (chopped finely)
2 cups tomatoes (chopped)
1 tsp cumin (ground)
1 tsp chili powder
1/2 cup fresh cilantro
Lime juice (use 2 limes)
1 package frozen chopped spinach (Use a 10oz bag.
Thaw and drain.)
8 collard green leaves

Directions
1. In a medium skillet, heat olive oil. Sauté
chicken, garlic, and onion for about 10 minutes,
or until cooked through.
2. Add in tomatoes, chili powder, cumin, lime
juice, and cilantro and let simmer for about 5
minutes.
3. Add in spinach and let simmer for an additional
5 minutes. Then remove from heat.
4. Quickly steam collard greens in a separate pan
for about 3 minutes, or until they become soft.
5. Wrap the chicken mixture in collard greens and
serve.

Nutritional Information
Been craving Mexican lately? Give these yummy
enchiladas a try. With 270 calories, 34 grams of

protein, 12 grams of fat, and only 4 grams of carbs per serving, this lunch is a great find.

Sweet Curry Chicken Salad
Makes 3 servings

Ingredients
8 oz. chicken breast (cubed)
2 tsp olive oil
1 stalk of celery (chopped)
1 small onion (diced)
1/2 cucumber (diced)
1/2 cup almonds (chopped)
2 apples (chopped)
1/2 tsp curry powder
4 cups baby romaine lettuce

Directions
1. Cook chicken, onion, and celery in a sauté pan thoroughly in heated olive oil for 5-10 minutes. Put aside to let cool.
2. Combine almonds, cucumber, apples, and curry powder in a mixing bowl with the cooled chicken mixture.
3. Best served over a bed of baby romaine lettuce.

Nutritional Information
Yes, another chicken salad. However, this one is packed with 42 grams of protein, 20 grams of fat, 37 grams of carbs, and sure to keep your taste buds pleased. At 450 calories per serving, this lunch will keep you full through dinner. Just pack in a Tupperware container and store in the refrigerator.

Orange Salad

Makes 4 servings

Ingredients
2 carrots (shredded)
3 cups romaine lettuce (chopped)
1 navel orange (each slice cut in half)
2 cups papaya (dried)
2 Tbsp. fresh ginger (shredded)
Lime juice (use 1 lime)
1-2 Tbsp. honey (taste to your liking)
1 Tbsp. olive oil
Black pepper
Sea salt

Directions
1. Mix the orange, carrots, lettuce, and papaya in a big salad bowl and set aside.
2. Combine the ginger, honey, lime juice, olive oil, pepper, and salt. Stir well. Toss this dressing with the salad and serve.

Nutritional Information
With only 125 calories per serving, your taste buds and waistline will thank you for this fiber-rich salad. Low in fat with only 4 grams, this recipe also boasts 2 grams of protein and 22 grams of carbs. Keep fresh in the refrigerator until lunch time. If you choose, keep the dressing separate and mix in to your liking.

Mediterranean Salad
Makes 4 servings

Ingredients
2 cups tomatoes (Sliced. Beefsteak or heirloom tomatoes work best.)
1 cup cucumber (peeled, chopped)
1/3 cup yellow bell pepper (diced)
1/4 cup radishes (sliced)
1/4 cup flat-leaf parsley (chopped)
1 clove of garlic (minced)
1 Tbsp. lemon juice
3 Tbsp. extra-virgin olive oil
2 cups baby spinach (torn up)
Black pepper and sea salt (to taste to your liking)

Directions
1. In a large salad bowl, mix together bell pepper, cucumber, radishes, tomatoes, and parsley.
2. Over the salad, sprinkle lemon juice, oil, and garlic. Mix well, and salt and pepper to taste. Lay salad over the baby spinach and serve.

Nutritional Information
Instead of cutting this recipe into 4 servings (120 calories per), cut it in half (240 calories per) and enjoy a healthy and filling lunch. Light and refreshing, enjoy this lunch at 2 grams of protein, 10 grams of fat, and 6 grams of carbs.

Berry Spicy Salad
Makes 2 servings

Ingredients
1 jalapeño pepper
4 Tbsp. lime juice
1/4 tsp cumin (ground)
4 Tbsp. olive oil
4 cups baby greens (mixed)
2 cups fresh blackberries or raspberries (or try 1 cup of each!)
1/4 cup red onion (sliced thinly)

Directions
1. Remove the seeds from the jalapeño and mince the pepper flesh.
2. In a blender, put the olive oil, lime juice, cumin, and 2 tsp of the minced jalapeño. Blend until smooth.
3. With the greens, berries, and onion, toss the dressing and serve. (If there is jalapeño left over, feel free to mix it in with your salad.)

Nutritional Value
This kickin' salad is far from ordinary. The combination of the sweet berries with the cut of the jalapeño makes for a party inside your mouth. At just over 300 calories, 2 grams of protein, 28 grams of fat, and 15 grams of carbs per serving, this lunch will help you get through the rest of your work day.

Pomegranate, Fennel, and Arugula Salad
Makes 4 servings

Ingredients
1 pomegranate
2 navel oranges (large)
1 cup fennel (sliced thinly)
4 cups arugula
4 Tbsp. olive oil
Black pepper (to taste)

Directions
1. Peel both oranges and cut each into 10-12 small pieces.
2. Scoop out seeds from the pomegranate and save.
3. In a large bowl, put orange pieces, pomegranate seeds, and arugula.
4. Dress the salad with olive oil and pepper as preferred.

Nutritional Information
Pomegranates, rich with antioxidants, make this salad on-of-a-kind. With only 200 calories, 24 grams of fat, 2 grams of protein, and 19 grams of carbs, enjoy this beneficial lunch.

Orange and Hazelnut Fennel Salad

Makes 6 servings

Ingredients
3 bulbs. s fennel
6 navel oranges
1/3 cup orange juice (fresh is best)
1 tsp hazelnuts (chopped finely)
1 Tbsp. fresh orange zest
2 Tbsp. extra-virgin olive oil

Directions
1. Slice the fennel bulb. s finely. Peel the oranges and carefully slice away the white membrane.
2. On desired amount of fennel, arrange oranges on top. Sprinkle with the hazelnuts. Then sprinkle with the oil and orange juice. Add a touch of zest to finish it off.

Nutritional Information
Low in calories at only 135 per serving, this salad also contains 5 grams of fat, 2 grams of protein, and 23 grams of carbs. Since the recipe yields quite a few servings, this is a great option to keep refrigerated for the week. Take only half a serving one day and use as a side salad with one of your favorite lunches.

Buffalo Burgers
Makes 4 servings

Ingredients
1 lb. buffalo (ground)
1 Tbsp. basil
1 Tbsp. oregano
1/2 red onion (chopped finely)
2 cloves of garlic (minced)
2 tsp black pepper

Directions
1. In a large mixing bowl, knead all ingredients together well.
2. Form meat into patties. On low heat, broil or grill, flipping often. Should take around 10 minutes.

Nutritional Information
Protein, protein, protein! With 285 calories, 27 grams of protein, 17 grams of fat, and only 3 grams of carbs per serving, these burgers are fabulous for lunches, and can be easily frozen to keep on-hand during the week. Pair with a side salad of your choosing!

Beef Lettuce Wraps

Makes 4 servings

Ingredients
1 bunch green onions (chopped)
2 tsp sesame oil (dark)
2 Tbsp. olive oil
1 lb. ground beef
1 yellow onion (large, chopped)
2 cloves of garlic (minced)
1 tsp coconut aminos
1/4 cup and 2 Tbsp. Paleo Hoisin Sauce
1 Tbsp. rice wine vinegar
1 can water chestnuts (chopped, drained)

Directions
1. Over medium heat, brown the ground beef in 1 Tbsp. of olive oil in a big skillet. Drain and put aside.
2. Keeping that skillet hot, add in the other 1 Tbsp. of olive oil and onions. Sauté the onions until translucent.
3. Then mix in the coconut aminos, garlic, Hoisin sauce, and rice wine vinegar. Stir well and cook for 1-2 minutes.
4. Then add green onions, water chestnuts, sesame oil, and the browned beef. Stir well and cook for another 2 minutes, allowing the green onions to slowly wilt.
5. Remove mixture from heat and place in a large bowl.
6. Spoon the mixture into lettuce leaves and roll up.

Nutritional Information

Another great way to enjoy the sensation of a wrap without the carbs! At 320 calories per serving, this beef delight is a terrific option for lunch. Enjoy with 35 grams of protein, 16 grams of fat, and 6 grams of carbs. Tip: Keep lettuce separate when you pack, as to only heat up the beef mixture. Then wrap up and dig in!

Paleo-Style BLT
Makes 1 serving

Ingredients
1 Paleo wrap
1/4 cup tomatoes (diced)
1/2 cup mustard greens
3 strips of bacon (cooked, broken into pieces)
2 Tbsp. Paleo mayo
1 Tbsp. sauerkraut
1 Tbsp. garlic powder
Black pepper, sea salt, and chili powder (to season to your liking)

Directions
1. Lay out your Paleo wrap.
2. Mix all other ingredients together in a bowl.
3. Spoon mixture in a line down the center of Paleo wrap. Serve.

Nutritional Value
Paleo wraps are a fast alternative to bread, and allow you to enjoy your favorite classics! Enjoy this one with 115 calories, 4 grams of protein, 5 grams of fat, and 15 grams of carbs per serving.

Ham Wrap
Makes 1 serving

Ingredients
4 leaves romaine lettuce
4 oz deli ham
1/2 medium carrot (shredded)
1 thin slice red onion (minced)
5 Tbsp. cilantro (raw)
1 serving of your favorite Paleo-friendly dressing
1/2 Tbsp. coconut oil

Directions
1. Heat coconut oil in a frying pan. Cook ham for about 5 minutes, or until a brownish color.
2. Lay out lettuce leaves. Put the carrot, onion, cilantro, and dressing on the leaves.
3. Lay the cooked ham atop the dressed lettuce leaves. Roll up and serve.

Nutritional Information
This easy lunch is under 260 calories per serving, packs 19 grams of protein, 8 grams of carbs, and 17 grams of fat. The saltiness of the ham paired with the juicy crunch of the lettuce makes for a treat. Eat warm or cold -- either way is great!

Thai Chicken Wraps

Makes about 2.5 servings

Ingredients
1 chicken breast (boneless, skinless)
12 lettuce leafs (bibb or romaine)
4 cabbage leafs (chopped thinly)
1 cup broccoli (raw, finely chopped)
1 large carrot (shredded)
3 green onions (sliced thinly)
1/3 cup fresh cilantro

Thai Sauce
1/4 cup almond butter
2 Tbsp. coconut aminos
2 Tbsp. lime juice
2 garlic cloves (minced)
1/4 cup water
(Mix all ingredients well in a bowl until smooth.)

Directions
1. Grill or cook chicken breasts. Dice into 1/2" cubes.
2. Lay out desired number of lettuce leafs.
3. Fill leaves with chicken, cabbage, broccoli, carrots, green onion, and cilantro.
4. Sprinkle with Thai Sauce.

Nutritional Information
This zesty lunch is packed with flavor and veggies. With 315 calories, 29 grams of protein, 13 grams of carbs, and 17 grams of fat, enjoy this recipe for a couple of meals!

Paleo Meat Sandwich
Makes 1 serving

Ingredients
2 lettuce leafs (large)
Thinly sliced deli meat (turkey, ham, chicken..)
1/2 avocado
1/2 tomato (sliced)
1/2 cup cucumber (chopped)
1 slice red onion
Black pepper and sea salt

Directions
1. Wash ingredients and let dry.
2. Lay out a slice of the meat of your choice. In a line, spread the avocado on one long end of the meat, and carefully add in the other ingredients. Sprinkle with salt and pepper to season.
3. Neatly roll the slice of meat around the fillings, and then roll a lettuce leaf around the meat. Complete for each lettuce leaf.

Nutritional Information
Okay, this isn't your typical sandwich, but just because you're sparing the carbs doesn't mean you're sparing the taste. Very easy to prepare, the sandwich roll-ups are perfect for lunch packing. With 230 calories, 13 grams of protein, 13 grams of carbs, and 14 grams of fat, play around with different meats to see which one is your favorite!

Chicken and Portobello Mushroom Sandwich

Makes 2 servings
Ingredients
4 portobello mushroom tops (large)
2 chicken breasts (small)
1-2 lettuce leafs
Tomato (2 thin slices)
1 Tbsp. coconut oil
Black pepper and sea salt (to season to your liking)

Directions
1. Preheat oven to 400F.
2. Cut stems off of Portobello mushrooms. Get as close to the mushroom top and you can.
3. Use a sheet on tin foil to line a baking tray for the mushrooms. Place mushrooms (rounded part facing up) on the tray and drizzle coconut oil. Sprinkle with black pepper and sea salt if you'd like. Cook for 10-15 minutes.
4. While the mushrooms cook: Cook or grill chicken breasts on medium heat for about 10 minutes, or until cooked through.
5. Once chicken and mushrooms have cooked, sandwich 1 chicken breast between two mushroom tops, adding in lettuce and tomato. Serve.

Nutritional Information
At around 320 calories per serving, this sandwich is an excellent lunch item. Juicy, flavorful, and easy to make, this recipe has 39 grams of protein, 7 grams of carbs, and 15 grams of fat. Easily re-heat at work!

Kale Crunch Salad
Makes 1-2 servings

Ingredients
1 bunch of kale (medium-size)
1 carrot (shredded)
1/2 cup golden beats (finely cut)
Lemon juice (use 1.5 lemons)
Lemon zest (use 1 lemon)
1 Tbsp. olive oil
Sea salt and black pepper
1/4 cup of your favorite chopped nuts (walnuts, almonds, pecans, etc.)

Directions
1. Thinly cut the kale leafs and place into a large bowl.
2. Add in carrots, beets, lemon juice and zest, olive oil, and salt and pepper. Stir well.
3. Allow salad to sit for 10-20 minutes so that the vegetables can soften a bit.
4. Top with the chopped nuts of your choice.

Nutritional Information
Kale is a great source of vitamins. At 370 calories, 11 grams of protein, 15 grams of carbs, and 33 grams of fat, this quick salad will keep you full and feeling good. Try with a piece of fresh fruit for dessert.

Radicchio-Wrapped Lemon-Basil Chicken Salad

Makes 4 servings

Ingredients
2 cooked chicken breasts (Boneless, skinless. Cut into small pieces.)
1 radicchio
2 stalks of celery (cut into small pieces)
1/4 cup basil (chopped)
2 Tbsp. olive oil
2 Tbsp. lemon juice
1 tsp garlic powder (or fresh minced garlic)
Sea salt and black pepper (to season to your liking)

Directions
1. Peel and separate the leaves from the radicchio, and let soak in cold water for a 1-2 minutes. Let them dry and set aside.
2. Mix together the celery, chicken, and basil.
3. In a separate, smaller bowl, mix together the garlic powder, olive oil, lemon juice, salt, and pepper.
4. Mix dressing in with the chicken salad.
5. Scoop a portion of the chicken salad into the radicchio wrap.

Nutritional Information
This is another quick and easy chicken salad recipe, but the radicchio sets it apart. The crispness of the radicchio complements the chicken salad wonderfully. At under 150 calories per serving, 14 grams of protein, 9 grams of fat, and only 1 gram of carbs, this wrap can become a staple lunch for you.

Turkey on Tapioca Bread
Makes 2 servings

Ingredients
1 cup tapioca flour
2 Tbsp. water
2 Tbsp. olive oil
3 eggs
Sea salt (to taste)
4oz of your favorite deli turkey
2 leafs of lettuce
2 slices of tomato

Directions
1. Heat olive oil in a skillet over medium heat. (This oil not included in ingredients.)
2. Mix flour, oil, water, eggs, and salt in a bowl and whisk until smooth; there shouldn't be any lumps.
3. Pour mix into the heated skillet to make one big flat bread.
4. Flip to other side when cooked to your liking. It should probably be browned a bit.
5. Remove bread from pan and let cool. Slice into rectangular pieces and assemble your mini sandwiches with turkey, lettuce, and tomato.

Nutritional Information
This recipe is tasty, simple, and fun to make. Almost like a big tortilla, this bread is just the right amount fluffy. This meal has 390 calories, 17 grams of protein, 22 grams of fat, and 32 grams of carbs per serving. Mix up the deli meat and accouterments for this versatile lunch!

Taco Salad

Makes 4-6 servings

Ingredients
1 lb. ground beef
1 packet taco seasoning
1 bag romaine lettuce (cut into small pieces)
1 bell pepper (large, any color)
1 can black olives (sliced)
1-2 tomatoes (seeded, diced)
1 cucumber (seeded, diced)
1 avocado (pitted, diced)
Your favorite salsa (no sugar added)

Directions
1. Over medium-high heat, brown the ground beef.
2. Add the taco seasoning and 1 Tbsp. of water to the skillet when the beef is totally brown. Stir until combined, then remove from heat.
3. While the beef is cooking: prepare all the veggies.
4. To serve, layer lettuce, beef, and veggies as you please. Mix in salsa as needed.

Nutritional Value
Protein, flavor, and iron rich, this simple lunch is fulfilling and portable. With around 250 calories, 30 grams of protein, 7 grams of carbs, and 12 grams of fat, try adding your favorite hot sauce or even a couple jalapeño peppers for more spice!

Cauliflower Rice with Sausage
Makes 5 servings

Ingredients
1 head cauliflower (cut into florets)
2 Tbsp. coconut oil
1/2 cup white onion
3-4 Tbsp. basil pesto
2 cups baby spinach
12 oz. Italian style chicken sausage (precooked)

Directions
1. In a bowl section of a food processor, place the cauliflower pieces. Pulse until cauliflower has become about the size of rice. (You may need to do this in shifts.)
2. Heat coconut oil in a big skillet over medium heat. Add the onions and sauté for 3-4 minutes. Then add in the cauliflower and stir to combine. Reduce the heat to medium-low, cover, and let it steam/cook for 5-8 minutes (until cauliflower is soft).
3. In a separate skillet, slice sausage into 1/2" coins and heat. Once heated through and have browned a bit, remove from heat and keep warm.
4. Mix 3 Tbsp. of pesto and the baby spinach into the cauliflower. Cook thoroughly until the spinach is wilted. Add salt and additional pesto if desired.
5. Serve the sausage over the cauliflower.

Nutritional Value
How cool is cauliflower rice? At only 170 calories, 13 grams of protein, 5 grams of carbs, and 11 grams of fat per serving, this quick lunch will have all the office

talking. If you're not a huge sausage fan, try this recipe with chicken or beef chunks. Yum!

Melon-Mint Shrimp Salad
Makes 4 servings

Ingredients
1 1/2 lb. medium shrimp (pre-cooked)
1/2 cup mint leaves
3 cups arugula
1 cup mango (fresh, cubed)
1 cup cantaloupe (fresh, cubed)
3 Tbsp. lemon or lime juice
1 tsp nutmeg
1 tsp cinnamon

Directions
1. Place all ingredients in a large bowl. Mix well.
2. Use lime or lemon juice as your dressing, or top off with your favorite, Paleo-friendly, balsamic dressing.

Nutritional Information
Fresh, crisp, and tangy don't even begin to describe all the flavor that this simple salad has to offer. At 270 calories, 40 grams of protein, 18 grams of carbs, and 4 grams of fat per serving, what's not to love?

Protein-Stuffed Avocado

Makes 1 serving

Ingredients
1 avocado
2-3 kale leaves
2-4oz of your favorite deli turkey (chopped up)
2 hard-boiled eggs (cut into quarters)
1/2 cucumber (cut into large coins)

Directions
1. Lay out the kale leaves in medium sized bowl. (When packing for lunch, simply lay leaves down directly in an appropriately-sized Tupperware container.)
2. Cut avocado in half, remove pit, and set one half aside to save. Place avocado in the middle of the kale leaves.
3. Stuff full the avocado with turkey.
4. Circle the sliced cucumbers and hard-boiled eggs around the avocado.
5. Serve or refrigerate.

Nutritional Information
With 310 calories, 15 grams of protein, 13 grams of carbs, and 23 grams of fat per serving, this quick meal is great for a busy day. Your brain and tummy will thank you!

Beef Curry
Makes 4 servings

Ingredients
1 lb. beef (cut into strips or chunks)
Curry sauce (try Dulcet Mild Indian Curry Sauce)
1/4 cup coconut milk
2 cloves of garlic
1 yellow onion (chopped)

Directions
1. Brown beef strips/chunks, garlic, and onions over medium-high heat for about 10 minutes, or until cooked through, and vegetables become soft.
2. Turn down heat to low, and add in enough curry sauce to fully cover each piece of meat.
3. Add in coconut milk. Stir.
4. Let cook for an additional 3 minutes.
5. Serve.

Nutritional Information
This is a fast, savory meal that will keep you coming back for more. Boasting 260 calories, 35 grams of protein, 4 grams of cards, and 11 grams of fat per serving, save the remainder of this delicious lunch for the rest of the week.

Bacon and Beef Chili
Makes 4 servings

Ingredients
1 lb. ground beef
7 strips of bacon (diced)
1 Tbsp. garlic powder
2 Tbsp. chili powder
2 Tbsp. paprika
1 tsp cayenne pepper
2 tsp cumin
2 red bell peppers (diced)
1 clove of garlic (large, minced)
1 small can tomato sauce
1 can roasted tomatoes
Grated cheese of your liking (not required)

Directions
1. Cook bacon over medium heat until crispy.
2. Mix in peppers and garlic, and cook for about 5 minutes.
3. Add in the ground beef and spices. Stir and cook until beef is browned.
4. Add in tomato sauce and roasted tomatoes.
5. Top off with grated cheese, or serve as is.

Nutritional Information
Easily re-heatable, this tasty lunch is quick to make and office-friendly. Full of protein (49 grams!) and with under 450 calories per serving, stay warm with and satisfied with this chili recipe, which also has 10 grams of carbs and 22 grams of fat

Trail Mix Alternative
Makes 3 servings

Ingredients
1/2 cup almonds (whole)
1/2 cup cashews (whole)
1/2 1/2 cup sunflower seeds (raw)
1/2 cup flax seeds (raw)
1/2 cup dried cranberries
1/2 cup dried blueberries
1/2 cup yellow raisins

Directions
1. Mix all ingredients in a bowl.
2. Separate into 2 plastic baggies.

Nutritional Information
Looking for a non-traditional lunch idea? Try this one on for size. With plenty of healthy fats (26 grams) and protein (15 grams), this mix is sure to keep you energized throughout the day. With 365 calories and 16 carbs per serving, change up the mix with other dried fruits, nuts, and seeds that suit your preferences.

Broccoli Pancakes

Makes 1-2 servings

Ingredients
1 head broccoli (cut in small pieces)
4 Tbsp. coconut flour
1 carrot (grated)
3 eggs
Sea salt and black pepper (to season to your liking)
1 clove of garlic (minced)
4 Tbsp. sunflower seeds
Fresh dill (about a handful, chopped)
1 Tbsp. olive oil

Directions
1. Mix all ingredients, except for olive oil, into a batter. Let sit for 10 minutes.
2. Heat olive oil in a medium-sized skillet over high heat.
3. When skillet is hot, reduce heat to medium. Spoon in the batter to form small (about silver dollar sized) pancakes.
4. Cook until one side of the pancake is browned a bit. Flip and cook other side until browned.
5. On a paper towel, place cooked pancake so that some of the oil absorbs.
6. Serve warm.

Nutritional Value
This is an excellent lunch option for vegetarians. Simple and fun, broccoli pancakes have 265 calories, 12 grams of protein, 13 grams of carbs, and 18 grams of fat per serving. Try eating them over a green salad!

CONCLUSION

Embracing the Paleo diet reaps long-term health benefits. Former research biochemist and author of The Paleo Solution -- The Original Human Diet, Robb Wolf, says that the Paleo diet is the healthiest way to eat because "it works with your genetics to help you stay lean, strong and energetic." Unlike today's modern diet of refined food, sugar, and trans fat, the Paleo Diet incorporates only lean proteins, fruits and vegetables, and healthy fats from seeds, nuts, fish oil, and olive oil.

Although the Paleo list for allowed foods isn't very long, there is plenty of delicious variety involved in Paleo meals, snacks, desserts, and beverages. This book's focus on quick and easy lunches for the working woman is a great example of just that. With 31 tasty, do-it-yourself recipes, this book is valuable literature for those with a health-conscious mindset and a tight schedule. From salads to sandwiches, soups to wraps, you are certain to find something here that piques your interest and taste buds. Providing serving size, a full list of ingredients and measurements, comprehensible directions, and practical nutritional information, this collaboration will save you time and worry when it comes to sticking to your Paleo aspirations.

39509397R10027

Made in the USA
Middletown, DE
17 January 2017